How to Deal With Anxiety

―――――

An interim guide

By Jennifer Hooper

How to Deal With Anxiety

An interim guide

A dynamic change for the waiting lists for treatments, improve mental and physical wellbeing, end your worry now

This book comes along at a time when Employer Assistance Programs Agencies' caseloads are on the increase, and there is a rising waiting list for psychological therapies on the NHS. When those on patient waiting lists can no longer wait for prolonged periods, this Interim Method TM, interim guideline on How to Deal With Anxiety can help effect a shift outside of the consulting room, where the majority of the work gets done by the patient. Jennifer Hooper Enterprise Pocket Book provide an opportunity for a different perspective of an interim, alternative, interventive process, as opposed to just simply waiting and enduring the timeline axis pressure of that "all important first" appointment at some time in the future. You can start your recovery preparation now.

Jennifer Hooper of Counselling PGDip Goldsmiths University had volunteered at Victim Support and was a Trustee Director at Hillingdon Women's Centre. She also was an Honorary Counsellor at Hestia Housing and at Southwark Psychological Services, GP Surgeries in South East London. She now has been in private practice since 2010 as a counsellor, psychotherapist, supervisor, coach, and critical incident debriefer, and has overseen other innovative projects in treatments and therapy. She has an interest in organic medicines, natural superfoods, and alternative therapy. She works seamlessly using a 'total field' of different psychotherapy modalities as a Clinical Recovery Specialist with low, moderate and more complex cases in her practice, underpinned by Energy Psychology, in Ruislip, Harley Street District, Kings Cross,

Marylebone, and tranquil locations. She does sessional work with individuals, couples, families, groups, Executive EAP sub-contracting, and Trauma sub-contracting.

Visit: http://www.allowyourselftogrow.co.uk/

COPYRIGHT MATERIAL

How to Deal With Anxiety

London, USA, Melbourne, New Zealand

To all those who believe in my work

Author of book: **Jennifer Hooper**

First Published in London, Great Britain: Self-published in 2017

Self Published by the author: Jennifer Hooper

Ruislip, Middlesex, Great Britain

http://www.allowyourselftogrow.co.uk/

Text copyright and front cover © Copyright Jennifer Hooper PGDip, BSc, FdD, 2017. All rights reserved. Reproduction, adaptation, or translation without permission is prohibited except as allowed under the International copyright laws. All the text, graphics, design, content, and other works not specifically mentioned herein are the copyrighted works of Jennifer Hooper.

Image on front cover: By Mopic, Illustrator, Vector Artist, Videographer

Although the author and publisher have made every effort to ensure that the information in this book was correct at press time, the author and publisher do not assume and hereby disclaim any liability to any party for any loss, damage, or disruption caused by errors or omissions, whether such errors or omissions result from negligence, accident, or any other cause.

In no event will the author and publisher be liable for any loss or damage including without limitation, indirect or consequential loss or damage, or any loss or damage whatsoever arising from loss of data or profits arising out of, or in connection with, the use of this book.

ALL INFORMATION AND MATERIALS AVAILABLE IN THIS BOOK IS PROVIDED "AS IS" FOR INFORMATION PURPOSE ONLY AND WITHOUT ANY WARRANTIES OF ANY KIND, EITHER EXPRESS OR IMPLIED, AND THE AUTHOR AND PUBLISHER DISCLAIMS ALL WARRANTIES OF ANY KIND, EITHER EXPRESS OR IMPLIED, INCLUDING WARRANTIES OF MERCHANTABILITY, FITNESS FOR A PARTICULAR PURPOSE, NON-INFRINGEMENT OF INTELLECTUAL PROPERTY OR ARISING FROM A COURSE OF DEALING, USAGE OR TRADE PRACTICE. IN NO EVENT SHALL THE AUTHOR AND PUBLISHER BE LIABLE FOR ANY DAMAGES WHATSOEVER (INCLUDING, WITHOUT LIMITATION, INDIRECT, SPECIAL, CONSEQUENTIAL OR INCIDENTAL DAMAGES OR THOSE RESULTING FROM LOST PROFITS, LOST DATA OR BUSINESS INTERRUPTION) ARISING OUT OF THE USE, INABILITY TO USE, OR THE RESULTS OF USE OF THIS BOOK, WHETHER BASED ON WARRANTY, CONTRACT, TORT OR ANY OTHER LEGAL THEORY AND WHETHER OR NOT ADVISED OF THE POSSIBILITY OF SUCH DAMAGES. IF YOUR USE OF THE MATERIALS OR INFORMATION IN THIS BOOK RESULTS IN THE NEED FOR SERVICING, REPAIR OR CORRECTION OF EQUIPMENT OR DATA, YOU ASSUME ALL COSTS THEREOF.

Every effort has been made to ensure that the information in this book is accurate. However, neither the publisher nor the author is engaged in rendering professional advice or services to the individual reader.

Always consult your doctor before embarking on any condition requiring a psychological assessment, medical treatment, or changing your diet. If you have any concern regarding nutrition or health matters, consult your doctor. While the information and guidance in this book are believed to be accurate and true at the time of publication, neither the author, nor publisher, nor distributor can guarantee results, nor accept any responsibility or liability for any damage or losses of any kind resulting from any advice or guidance given in this guide, be it from the author, any person or third party mentioned in this guide, any product or listing or mention, whether directly or indirectly.

Please be aware that this book was written in the UK where products and websites are concerned, there is, therefore an unavoidable UK bias. No refunds can be given on that basis. Readers must check any website links quoted. Updates will be included in subsequent editions. Successful treatments or therapeutic value are the responsibility of the reader of this book.

A catalogue reference number for this book is available from the British Library

ISBN 978-0-9957544-0-9
Hooper, Jennifer,
Self Published

Preface

What to do if someone ever says 'you cannot write.... ...' as I experienced in 2016-17. Write a book, even write poetry.

"You cannot write"
I shan't give up without a fight
To show you with all my might.
Writing is not simply for Thee
As an academic exercise for a fee

I took to the task when you said:
'Give it up'
I was not about to simply just stop
With all that privileged power
And just cower

And not be known for:
Talent.
(c) Jennifer Hooper 2017

Book Review

This is a fantastic book for anyone that struggles with stress and anxiety. The book outlines strategies to manage and cope with your anxiety for Free.

What's amazing about the book is how comprehensive it is with such brevity. It is a handy reference guide to living a simple and anxiety-free life."

Each piece of instruction by outlined Jennifer is clear and to the point. You will find little to no fluff in this book.

This book is written for those who is constantly overwhelmed and struggling with daily anxiety and stress, and confined in negative thinking. It's also for those who need to manage their inner lives to maximize happiness, peace of mind, and productivity. I would highly recommend this book as an antidote to anxiety.

How to Deal With Anxiety by Jennifer Hooper have worked really well for me and I recommend this book to anyone looking for inner peace.

Review by Amanda Timothy

Acknowledgements

My sons and granddaughter -- lights in my life.

Lecturers and teachers that noticed my free-spirited learning style and supported me: Mrs. Macintyre at St Anslem's primary school, Manoj N., and Maggie B. at RACC Adult College, and Lynne H. at Goldsmiths University.

Forward

The Interim Method

The Interim Method TM explained, is a form of psychotherapy that is, a mastery of a motivational inner critic practice of self-care, in a nutshell. This idea was born out of the current state of the mental health and wellbeing industry being overwhelmed with treatment waiting lists that is being largely seen as a growing problem that needs a solution nowadays. The Interim Method TM places a therapeutic focus on what you can do before during and after treatments that can place you in control alongside medical and psychological interventions. Mastering this form of psychotherapy could change your life and the current waiting for treatments system, placing emphasis on building the strength and construction of your inner critic in a sustaining way and employing creativity for development to take place.

Table of contents

1. How to Deal with Anxiety 1
2. Dealing With Anxiety - A Look Back 5
3. Dealing with Anxiety in our Everyday Life 7
4. Rules to Consider While Dealing with Anxiety 9
5. The Easiest Way to Deal with Anxiety 11
6. Dealing with Anxiety for Free 13
7. Dealing with Anxiety - Step by Step 15
8. Strategies for Dealing with Anxiety 17
9. Tips On How To Deal with Anxiety Better 19
10. Common Questions about Dealing with Anxiety 21
11. Book Description 27

HOW TO DEAL WITH ANXIETY

Dealing with anxiety will be a life event unlike any other, and you need to plan respectively. You must not approach this like something you pursued in the past. If you are looking to thrive with managing anxiety, you ought to draw on your resources for the distinctive challenges that dealing with anxiety presents.

It is also reasonable to accept that anxiety can be normal until it affects you in an abnormal way, like a disorder, socially or becomes generalised as being more anxious than usual.

We hope to explore the voyage to dealing with anxiety fruitfully. We can prepare you for a different level of success. Please consider some thoughts one must think of before seeking to manage anxiety. Before you attempt on dealing with anxiety, you ought to gauge and make certain that managing anxiety is the right fit for your work balance and lifestyle.

The easiest way to make that assessment is to ask yourself the following questions:

Do you want to recover?

Are you willing to beat it?

Are you determined?

If you replied "yes" to these specific questions, then presumably dealing with anxiety is the right match for you. Well done for committing to the plunge of managing your anxiety!

Following are some suggestions to get you on your way:

- Daily Brisk Exercise

    - Taking a walk at lunch time for 20 minutes, 3-4 times a week is comparable to psychotherapy according to some researchers and psychologists from the University of Illinois.

    - Performing brisk exercises daily i.e. quick and energetic exercises is a critical part of the equation that a person attempting to reduce anxiety should try - and what's more, it is free! If you are accustomed to performing brisk exercises on a regular basis, managing your anxiety would be less difficult. If you have limited mobility, your local nurse or General Practitioner might be able to guide you on exercises you can do at home sitting or lying down.

- Eating healthy

    - Eating healthily every day keeps your body in prime condition, fortify your immune system and increase your health bar which helps to keep you productive; focus your energy on meeting your objectives. Carving time to eat healthily keeps your body and mind sharp, focus and alert which helps keep your body in a "willing and ready state" to try out new things; new treatment.

- Being aware

    - Being aware of your body and your reactions to situations is another strategy you can employ to manage your anxiety. You'd recognize already that you need to be in control in order to reduce anxiety. Individuals who are unable to be in control regularly will, unfortunately, encounter challenges with dealing with anxiety.

- Considering you recognize that you are in the right mindset to reduce anxiety, we can explore a handful of preliminary practices that an individual dealing with anxiety will already be doing. Use that opportunity to incorporate these practices into your routine because this will make the challenge to reduce anxiety easier.

- Managing anxiety requires more than getting up one evening to say, "Oh, I need to deal with my anxiety." Sure, that is a starting step, however, to pursue any benefit with managing anxiety, you should first prepare mentally.

DEALING WITH ANXIETY - A LOOK BACK

Nothing good comes easy, so does dealing with anxiety. If you are trying to deal with your anxiety, you must know that the road to success would be difficult and challenging; physically and mentally. Dealing with anxiety requires a lot of effort which discourages people from the onset; if it was painless, it'd be a feat everyone would accomplish easily. Studies have shown that people who make the decision to manage anxiety in most cases end up not doing it.

Congratulations for being the type of individual that takes the plunge. It is probable that people who struggled to manage anxiety and fell short most likely did not properly prepare themselves. By going over the opening questions to determine your readiness when it comes to managing anxiety, you have subconsciously acknowledged what is needed to succeed.

Ask yourself again: Do you truly want to recover? Reflect on that question carefully, as those who have proven to reduce anxiety share a common but significant trait; - they are resilient about their wants and goals – determined at all costs to reduce anxiety. You also have to become resilient if you expect to make your desire of managing anxiety a reality.

It is very important to be sure you have the zeal to succeed in managing your anxiety. Do you want to recover? As previously stated, trying to recover is more than simply stating out your desire – dealing with anxiety, as there exist a major difference between thinking and doing. Undoubtedly, you will need a lot of willpower to persevere should you embark on the journey of managing your anxiety.

Jennifer Hooper

Studies show that individuals who have had great success dealing with anxiety all did something – Acknowledgement. Successful people acknowledged exactly what was required, and were surely able to face it directly. What can we all pick from that? When you set your mind and prepare your body to Deal with anxiety, your chances of successfully dealing with anxiety increases exponentially as you put yourself in the right position to tackle anxiety successfully.

Dealing with anxiety has a physical quality to it. Positively, any action for which you prepare in advance for usually ends with a beneficial result. You will find the strength needed and the right set of mind that will help you achieve your goal.

Do not dwell on 'what if' scenarios. Managing anxiety necessitates one to be optimistic, resilient and focused. We realize this and have been able to review the specific steps needed for managing anxiety so we can appreciate our forthcoming accomplishments.

You need to know that both being aware and taking action are not just necessary, but are also accomplishments in their own right. When your mind speaks negatively e.g. tells you that dealing with anxiety is impossible, just consider the fact that your mind will do anything to avoid a change even if it has to speak negatively, the fact that you are aware and taking action is enough to drive your mind crazy and that knowledge should give you the needed boost you need to attain your goal. Now that our mind is in sync with our self and goals, let us explore what is needed to successfully manage anxiety.

DEALING WITH ANXIETY IN OUR EVERYDAY LIFE

Dealing with anxiety may not be something that you opt to do daily, but if you look at the effects of managing anxiety, you can blend that into your daily life. The truth is, managing anxiety includes positive side effects that will benefit other areas of life.

In actuality, dealing with anxiety requires a shift in your logic. The development of a resilient quality, which is essential to manage anxiety, will alter your whole life. You will find that being resilient when dealing with your anxiety, will help you act resiliently in your everyday life. This will be the defining success of dealing with anxiety that many people do not consider.

When you look at dealing with anxiety as a lifestyle instead of a goal, you will find it easier to adopt the habits that enhance your success. The change in your daily regimen and mindset has a bigger purpose beyond achieving a single goal.

An example is an individual need to increase his/her confidence. This is not just an attribute that is essential to reduce anxiety but for all areas of life.

The truth is that learning to manage your anxiety helps you in all aspects of your life. This truth will be undeniable as soon as you start managing anxiety. Things such as performing brisk exercises, eating healthily, coupled with being aware and taking actions, all necessitate skills that you can use throughout life. Managing anxiety creates numerous useful skills before you even reach your goals.

If you will think back to when we first began the voyage of managing our anxiety, you may remember being presented with the following questions:

Do you want to recover?

Are you willing to beat it?

Are you determined?

You may find out that these same questions can be applied to other areas of your life. These may create endless possibilities of positive impact on lifestyle choices as you work on managing your anxiety.

Definitely, no one will ever say dealing with anxiety is a painless process - it is undeniable. You need to be resilient and confident to contemplate managing anxiety. Just be mindful that dealing activities need time and commitment. If realizing huge successes were as painless as snapping your fingers, everybody would be doing it.

The most dedicated people will see this goal to the end. You can become one of those people. If you will allow your mind to become reasonable, you will find the voyage an exhilarating one. Good for you for taking it on!

RULES TO CONSIDER WHILE DEALING WITH ANXIETY

As we have already examined, dealing with anxiety takes quite a bit out of an individual. They have to be resilient, confident, and reasonable. While some individuals possess these attributes others are not so lucky. The reality, however, is that getting ready for the enormous change and impact that managing anxiety will bring, can ultimately strip those attributes from you.

Following are some guidelines you ought to follow that will help you nurture these attributes as you begin to manage your anxiety.

Priming yourself for dealing with anxiety takes some energy. Many of these standards will be entrenched in your head during this time frame. Since you will most likely be spending a few weeks on the art of these tasks, you should ensure you have ample time to devote some energy on these rules.

If you are passing through an anxious episode, you must remember to breathe correctly; in through your nose and out through your mouth. This can help regulate the fight and flight response. This is just one of many results that this rule will yield. In addition, you should feel calm, especially when the time comes to actually reduce anxiety.

Keep a diary of your intrusive thoughts in order to analyse them – the harmony or anomaly! This is an ideal rule to follow as it parallels to eating healthy. This can act as a strategy to challenge the anxiety as your body absorbs good nutrition. If you see yourself as confident in taking one step at a time, then it will be straightforward for you to follow these guidelines in your life.

You need to consistently keep your focus concentrated on being in control of the anxiety as a 'thing.' This will likely challenge you to become much more committed when you do this work, and the commitment is absolutely worth it. This also helps you get through the day.

Just remain focused on your recovery - this means resting properly, which will allow you to notice what has changed about your thoughts, feelings, and behaviours over time.

Dealing with anxiety is much more than worrying about 'what if' scenarios. Even though any individual can attempt to manage anxiety, it takes one who is determined and resilient to really reach the objective of managing anxiety.

After making a promise to be fully prepared, it will be your duty to keep at it! Even at those times when you want to stop, you need to push on -Winners never quit, quitters never win! Did you remember when you answered these questions?

Do you want to recover?

Are you willing to beat it?

Are you determined?

You proved you were resilient, confident, and reasonable by simply saying yes to each of these three questions. As you attempt to manage your anxiety, these virtues should benefit you. Remember the main rules: perform brisk exercises 3-4 times a week, eat healthily, relax, and be in control of 'it.' In turn, you should experience a positive mental and emotional shift in no time!

THE EASIEST WAY TO DEAL WITH ANXIETY

There are numerous strategies that an individual can use to Deal with anxiety. At this point, you ought to know that planning is the key to becoming successful. Allocating enough time to whatever step you are working on, even to the simplest technique to reduce anxiety will do wonders for you.

You are now really ready to get into the task at hand. But, first, we will cover a few beneficial habits. This way you are as primed as possible when you start working to manage your anxiety. First, you should work on the steps we have already discussed to manage anxiety: light exercise, healthy eating and to be in control of the feelings leading to anxiety. Altogether, these tips create a solid core for your learning.

Preparing to reduce anxiety is absolutely vital, and cannot be emphasized enough. It permits you to fully engage. Furthermore, it certainly gives you more motivation using these three beneficial practices essential for dealing with anxiety. You should find that you can utilize your greatest effort possible.

Please be sure to prevent rejecting your plan by using a form called GAD7 Anxiety Test Questionnaire. It is normally used by Health Practitioners but you might find it useful checking your own scores or being able to give it to a clinician. You should be able to find a form here http://www.phqscreeners.com/select-screener/41. However, never rule out seeing a General Practitioner if you need to, or a qualified Health Practitioner.

This way, you will prevent needing to accomplish things the problematic way. Resolve to make preparations the painless way so you experience all of the following benefits: feeling calmer, feeling positive, feeling good about yourself. Furthermore, you will benefit in additional ways like creating good energy, controlling thoughts and feelings, as well as feeling good about your inner self.

If you choose to invest the time to manage with anxiety, you may find that it is a lot easier than you anticipated. The right planning trains you to become totally ready. This results in releasing tension and a chance of feeling much happier. These benefits guide you to effectively manage anxiety. That being said, do not merely race through all of the work since all these benefits are equally vital.

Many individuals mistakenly believe that it is problematic, or even impractical, to become a resilient individual in an increasingly complex society. Typically, it just takes one who is ready and willing to practice the art to become resilient, confident and reasonable to ultimately go through the preparatory phases. If you will completely commit to avoiding short-cuts in the preparation period and finish all of the work involved, then you are strategically positioned to reduce anxiety.

In closing, the simplest technique on this course to managing anxiety is to follow all of the work laid out here. Ultimately, cutting corners is definitely not worth risking a positive outcome and should be avoided when managing anxiety. You need to devote your time on the preliminary phase of the journey since it will make you more successful. The truth is, setting aside a few days or weeks to create new ideas about managing anxiety, and learning how to practice the new behaviours is actually not a lot of time to make the preparations for such a life-changing event that will reframe your skills in dealing with anxiety. So, make the promise, put forth the required amount of time, and you should be managing anxiety in no time!

DEALING WITH ANXIETY FOR FREE

You are not totally wrong if you believe that it costs a lot of money to Deal with anxiety, managing your anxiety can actually be for free if you follow the guide layout in this book. The key thing you ought to do when you seek to manage anxiety is to remove any existing opinions you may possibly have relating to what it will be like.

There are a few fundamental guidelines for using your Pocket Book that will help you balance your goals of dealing with anxiety. You can practice breathing techniques yourself, but always see your General Practitioner for a check-up. Anytime you focus your energy on relaxation, you facilitate your consciousness to focus on what you ought to be doing so it becomes conscious - a new pattern. This does not cost you any anything. Bear in mind, that performing brisk exercises daily, eating healthy, coupled with being in control of the anxiety, are areas that are most important.

There are other measures you can do in order to avoid spending cash. Look for opportunities to enjoy your own space and get closer to nature as much as you can. Enjoy your time with friends, family or funded community groups. That is a simple choice when your goals are your focal point.

Socialising with others who care about you and that have your best interests at heart might enhance your wellbeing and this need not be expensive. Once again, there is a multitude of inexpensive hobbies you can pursue to help realize the final goals to guide you through anxiety.

The key thing that you ought to do is to consistently be concentrating on your goal. By simply looking at decisions through the filter of your goal, you will recognize which thoughts and feelings are not serving you.

Jennifer Hooper

Anytime you put forth the time to recognize the patterns that need to change or be interrupted, you should feel calm, which is one of the critical signs that you are managing anxiety. Engaging in brisk exercise daily does not require spending a lot of money. Eating healthy motivates you to control thoughts and feelings. Controlling your thoughts and feelings also does not require a huge amount of money. There is a biochemical aspect to managing anxiety. It can be done very affordably with determination, but medical advice and psychological assessment might also be needed.

Finally, devote more effort on the plan, coupled with how you ought to be in control. Do not allow yourself to become overwhelmed by doing too much at once - take things step by step. Be reasonable with the tasks in the plan and notice your own resources being enabled as you go along.

Nevertheless, you need to be determined and simply think about your critical plan to reduce anxiety. Your feelings will play a large role when looking at the effort required, but effort means activity, and activity usually results in reduced anxiety. Focusing on all of these steps is the key to dealing with anxiety. By simply recognizing this, you ought to be able to engage the process and make a great deal of progress toward executing your plan.

DEALING WITH ANXIETY - STEP BY STEP

At this point, we know clear which kind of person it takes to effectively deal with anxiety. We have also learned more about all the virtues that one needs in order to manage anxiety. So now we can get started with what we set to achieve.

Undoubtedly, the preliminary step is making sure that you are engaging in some type of brisk exercise each day since this can determine your readiness to reduce anxiety. You ought to think of briskly exercising daily as such: no person can truthfully manage anxiety quickly without regular exercise. This step is crucial to be able to manage your anxiety. It will also result in you feeling calmer and more positive. When you begin your daily brisk exercise, you will have a lot to gain and absolutely nothing to lose!

Furthermore, eating healthy is required to manage anxiety. There are clearly numerous benefits for this. Creating good energy, though, is considered the most helpful benefit of dealing with anxiety. Without creating good energy, you can expect that it will be extremely difficult to effectively manage anxiety.

The additional benefits of eating healthy, as it relates to managing anxiety, include more control over your thoughts and feelings, as well as simply feeling good about yourself. In actuality, if you are not executing some kind of step towards feeling good about yourself, then it may be cumbersome to accomplish anything considerable. Even if you choose against dealing with anxiety, then you still should definitely contemplate ventures that result in feeling good about yourself.

You should prepare for managing anxiety in under a few weeks once you start following these steps. But remember this is a process so it could take a bit longer. Generally, days, if not a few weeks, will be the typical amount of time that people schedule in order to prepare to reduce anxiety. Reflect on these averages when you are setting your timelines.

A different factor that will be necessary to help you become successful with managing anxiety is being in control of 'it.' You might have had no reason to focus on being in control until now, so the change might be difficult initially, being in control ought to help you get through the day, and may be beneficial to your preliminary efforts and the action phase of secondary preparations. Being in control also pushes you to notice what has changed about your thoughts, feelings, and behaviours over time and release tension, which in turn pushes you to manage anxiety.

Remember, within the first few days and weeks, you ought to start exercising, eating healthy, and also devoting energy to being in control. Ideally, all of these activities should work jointly to get you prepared to manage anxiety. A great suggestion is to mark a fixed date you decide your preparations and schedule your time based on that. It should present you with a legitimate perspective. If you follow that guidance, start exercising briskly every day and eat healthily, then you will be prepared to manage anxiety in no time!

STRATEGIES FOR DEALING WITH ANXIETY

When you make the decision to deal with your anxiety, you may become curious in certain strategies to make certain that you are addressing your goal in a reasonable manner. There are definitive requirements to successfully managing anxiety. These requirements are related to qualities, and also attributes, that one holds.

You need to be devoted to the process if you want to successfully manage your anxiety. So, an individual who is doubtful, or otherwise sceptical, will not become as successful as they could really be. These virtues are found in individuals who might have said "no" when presented with the question:

Do you want to recover?

If you hope to manage anxiety, a few virtues are required. Being resilient is an absolute requirement. If you hope to accomplish your desire of managing anxiety and ultimately be a resilient individual, then you will need to gradually become confident.

The secret to becoming victorious at managing anxiety is getting ready in advance, and also finishing all of the steps toward managing anxiety. Anyone can claim that they wish to manage anxiety. In addition, pretty much any individual can succeed at worrying about 'what if' scenarios. But, managing anxiety is bigger than that. The time to concentrate on tactics came with the preparatory phases. As for many ventures in life, if you are hoping to thrive, then be sure you prepare.

You now know one aspect of managing anxiety requires daily exercise. This should not be a major deal when compared to managing anxiety. However brisk exercise is very vital when you reduce anxiety.

Eating healthy should be the standard as it is the absolute key for overall success to managing your anxiety. Eating healthy is vitally important because of the tasks involved.

Being aware might not seem like a major thing, but it certainly is. When trying to deal with your anxiety, you will need the learning which you invested time on during preparation. Your preparation will show what you will do differently, and how things may change.

The strategies to dealing with anxiety will benefit you in most aspect of life than just the desire to manage anxiety. Each step ultimately includes a multitude of great benefits that will complement other areas in your life. Do you realise that? It is straightforward to figure out that feeling calmer is not only a benefit to managing anxiety but also a benefit for life in general. Similarly, creating good energy is well-known to benefit many areas of life. Even getting through the day will become beneficial in addition to dealing with anxiety. Other than becoming a resilient individual, some people might also appreciate how managing anxiety improves their way of living in general.

When you implement the tactics and strategies needed to manage anxiety, you will find your present attributes greatly improved. Any resilient person should become much more resilient. Any confident person is likely to be much more confident and any reasonable person should become much more reasonable. This is why there is definitely no better time to begin than now! Tap into your personal development so you can master these tactics better and better.

TIPS ON HOW TO DEAL WITH ANXIETY BETTER

Dealing with anxiety may sometimes be perceived as a huge sacrifice, but there are ways to make your way of living a little more manageable when you are attempting to manage your anxiety. Following are a handful of tips for dealing with anxiety that may prove beneficial to you.

- Already discussed in the process of managing anxiety was the importance of daily brisk exercise. It is vital, that when you are exercising, that you also remember to breathe correctly. This will help regulate the fight and flight response. This is essential, not just when getting ready for dealing with anxiety, but in additional areas as well.

- You should also recognize that eating healthy is important. It can get problematic to do on your own. Often, an effective technique and a strategy for dealing with anxiety are to keep a diary about your thoughts especially after you eat, and to analyse them at a later date. This should grant you more incentive to eat healthy as you make preparations to reduce anxiety, and take professional advice and guidance.

- Furthermore, understand that when dealing with anxiety it needs you to be actively in control of it. Therefore, be sure you are getting proper rest. It is beneficial to remain focused on your recovery.

Reading this book on How to Deal With Anxiety will guide you to secure a lot of benefits, especially as more time goes by. Anytime you reduce anxiety, you will have the following benefits:

- You will feel calmer and more positive while exercising.

- As long as you are eating healthy, you should be full of energy.

- Eating healthy also allows you to be in better control of your thoughts and feelings.

- By simply preparing to reduce anxiety, you can begin to be in control and will get through the day because of it.

- Being in control also will help you notice what has changed about your thoughts, feelings, and behaviours over time.

There will be some special benefits that take place when managing anxiety is underway. Over time, feeling good about yourself will contribute to an improved way of living beyond the anxiety. Similarly, being in control contributes to successfully getting through the day if you are determined. To reap the additional benefits, following are some more guidelines that will help you accomplish your goal of managing anxiety.

When you follow the guidance you find here, you will be on the path to managing anxiety. Be sure to allow yourself days or a few weeks to prepare. Having a suitable period of time to prepare will be crucial.

However, these guidelines are merely a starting point. When you are finished reviewing this information, you will recognize everything that is required to reduce anxiety. Apply these reflections on becoming more positive, and you will be able to get going in no time.

COMMON QUESTIONS ABOUT DEALING WITH ANXIETY

At this point, you should be informed of the measures you must take to deal with anxiety. Let's say you identify a question that has not been addressed, do not fret! Following are two typical questions that surface with managing anxiety:

Is it viable to reduce anxiety for free?

Commonly, it is viable to manage anxiety for free. It would be overkill to put forth a lot of cash preparing to manage anxiety. Following are some guidelines to manage expenses.

- You can practise breathing techniques yourself.

- Look for opportunities to relax in your own space, and to experience nature as much as you can.

- Socialize with others who care about you and that have your best interests at heart. This might enhance your wellbeing and this need not be expensive.

- You might need to see your General Practitioner or a Health Care Practitioner for a check-up or if you find you are struggling in dealing with your anxiety.

A different question that usually comes up when a person is preparing to manage anxiety is relating to the typical "rules" to consider while managing anxiety. Following are a handful of rules to keep in mind:

- While exercising, remember to breathe correctly. This will help regulate the fight and flight response.

- Typically, eating healthy will be vital when managing anxiety. This should enhance the strategy for dealing with anxiety from a biochemical perspective.

- While you focus on being in control, be sure to remain focused on your recovery. This includes getting adequate rest.

You have begun the initial steps toward managing anxiety by reading more about it. Undoubtedly, more questions will surface. A different way you can benefit yourself may be by tackling this objective with a companion who have similar goals or anyone in your network of family or friends that you feel comfortable talking to about it.

At times a "buddy system" can be a beneficial solution when tackling an ambition that requires a resilient and confident personality. Even though you might ultimately manage anxiety independently, it is beneficial to accompany someone upon a parallel voyage to discuss challenges as they arise. Be mindful to choose like-minded friends and avoid people who are sceptical or doubtful, since they can drive you away from reaching your objectives. However, known disorders or any illness would need medical treatment and possibly psychological assessment.

Remember these questions you had answered just a moment ago?

Do you want to recover?

Are you willing to beat it?

Are you determined?

So, you have answered yes to the questions that determined you have the most effective nature to thrive at managing anxiety. Seeking advice and psychological assessment is always the best practice and ethically framed by government agencies, but sometimes a medicine may need to take precedent over organic treatments. However, you now have a set of tools using your own resources to thrive at dealing with anxiety that you can use in addition to professional advice and guidance in order to succeed. For more details refer to links below.

Pocket Book on dealing with anxiety!

QUICK REFERENCE

Suggestions to get you on your way – Page 1

Those who are successful have one share a significant trait – Page 5

Benefits – Page 7

Rules – Page 9

GAD7 Anxiety Test Questionnaire – Page 11

Tips – Page 19

Links:

http://www.acas.org.uk/media/pdf/l/a/Promoting_positive_mental_health_at_work(SEPT2014).pdf

https://www.functionalmedicine.org/What_is_Functional_Medicine/AboutFM/

https://www.gov.uk/government/uploads/system/uploads/attachment_data/file/551502/Eatwell_Guide_booklet.pdf

http://www.phqscreeners.com/select-screener/41

Jennifer Hooper

Note from the author:

If you have enjoyed this book, I would greatly appreciate it, if you could leave an honest Review on Amazon.

Go to the Amazon website and you can type this code into the url: B06XKBGCR3

Reviews are very important for us authors, and it only takes a minute for a post.

Thank you.

How to Deal With Anxiety – an interim guide

We want to be calmer. We also want to feel good about ourselves, and we want to deal with anxiety!

We can achieve ALL of these goals with the newest release from Jennifer Hooper, Clinical Recovery Director at Jennifer Hooper Enterprise, called *How to Deal with Anxiety*. Based on these exciting teachings, you will learn about all the dramatic benefits of feeling calmer and more positive.

This book is built around a very clear, concept: be happier.

It is not just about feeling better about yourself. Having a great way of living, in general, is linked to managing anxiety. This is because with hard work we have learned how to become resilient in an ever-changing global economy.

In this book, we look at practical ways you can improve your own way of living in general, starting with awareness. This book will also look at other steps that can be taken to support this goal, from preparing mentally to planning to become successful in managing your anxiety over a lifetime that can sometimes include major events. Even the choices you make about lifestyle can have an impact on your way of living in general, as well as anxiety levels that may be fluctuating or freezing at certain levels.

In *How to Deal with Anxiety*, we will cover all the basics, giving you everything you need to know to successfully manage anxiety before, during and after medical or psychological interventions. But if you want to try a better way, this could be it.

Jennifer Hooper

Testimonials

I first met Jennifer during a series of family therapy sessions. I felt that she quickly understood the family dynamics and allowed my children to speak and be heard. I hadn't realised before then how little they had been heard over the years. Several years later the benefits are still being felt as they took to heart what she said and they stood their ground. I then went to Jennifer for an extended period of personal therapy sessions. Again I found her to be extremely helpful. She helped me "wake up," make some changes and gave me the strength (despite the fear) to see them through. Life is much better for me now and I'll always be grateful. Over the years I've seen (I think) around 6 therapists and she is streets ahead. I can't recommend Jennifer highly enough. JH. Insurance/Finance

Jennifer has worked with me for just under 2 years and within that time she has supported me and helped me develop the tools I need to turn my life around. I met Jennifer at one of the most difficult times in my life; she showed me there was light, that this was not the end, but the beginning of a brighter and better future. Jennifer's guidance has helped me to think more positively and become a more confident person. I have seen other counsellors before, but this was different. I am now looking forward to the future instead of living in the past. Thank You, Jennifer! Miss E Teacher

My husband and I had sessions for two years. It helped us grow from being angry and not communicating effectively with each other to now being happy. Jennifer gave us tools to help improve our relationship with each other and others around us. J. Teacher